IMAGES
of America

ALEXANDRIA BAY

This panorama of the Upper Bay of Alexandria Bay was taken in the late 1800s. Note the foundation for the Church of the St. Lawrence in the right foreground. The church cornerstone was laid on October 8, 1887.

IMAGES
of America

ALEXANDRIA BAY

Thomas F. Folino

ARCADIA
PUBLISHING

Library of Congress Catalog Card Number: 2004102491

For all general information contact Arcadia Publishing at:
Telephone 843-853-2070
Fax 843-853-0044
E-mail sales@arcadiapublishing.com
For customer service and orders:
Toll-Free 1-888-313-2665

Visit us on the Internet at www.arcadiapublishing.com

ALEXANDRIA

Scale 1½ inches to the mile

This map, published by C. K. Stone Publishers of Philadelphia in 1864, was taken from "actual surveys of S. N. & D. G. Beers and Assistants," according to the atlas it was found in, entitled *New Topographical Atlas of Jefferson County, New York.*

CONTENTS

ACKNOWLEDGMENTS

There are many organizations and individuals to whom I owe my gratitude. It is through their generous sharing of materials and images, which appear inside these covers, that this book was made possible.

The town of Alexandria historian's office, the Thousand Islands Sun, the Thousand Islands Bridge Authority, the Alexandria Township Historical Society, and the Alexandria Bay Fire Department have each made significant contributions. Photographers David Putnam, Jim Spencer, Addison F. Vars III, and Tom Weldon extended great generosity in granting use of their images. Loans from the personal photograph collections of Tad and Kira Clark, Tamara Cavallario Quinn, Hunter Grimes III and Martha Grimes, Shane Sanford, Jeanne Roy Snow, and Frances Taitt have served to further enhance these pages. Assistance from Greta M. Slate, town historian, was invaluable.

A very special thank-you is extended to Hazel Simpson, town historian emeritus, whose ceaseless devotion to the preservation of our village history has enriched this publication, and our heritage, immeasurably. And finally, I wish to honor posthumously the many anonymous photographers of the past who, by capturing the moment, have left an indelible record of our rich village history. To them, as to all of the aforementioned, I extend my sincere and heartfelt appreciation.

This book is dedicated to the memory of the author's parents, Anthony and Carmella Folino, whose choice in making Alexandria Bay their home became his good fortune. The Folinos are seen here in 1933, the year they were wed.

INTRODUCTION

From the time of its inception as a tiny lumbering and shipping community in 1818 to its present-day status as a prominent vacation destination, Alexandria Bay's history has been governed strongly by its location on the banks of the St. Lawrence River. Situated in the heart of the Thousand Islands, it has earned the nickname "the Venice of America."

Calwallader Child happened upon the site in 1804, while surveying a road for landowner James D. LeRay. Seeing its possibilities, he recommended it to LeRay as a possible port to serve a growing lumber trade. However, it was not until 1818 that Edmund Tucker surveyed it for LeRay, who then erected a tavern and warehouse and named the new village after his son, Alexander.

Initially, growth was slow, as its inhabitants numbered 164 by 1848. The 1866 edition of Benjamin Child's *Gazetteer and Business Directory of Jefferson County* estimated the population to be, by that time, only 336.

In 1848, Charles Crossman opened the first hotel, catering to fishermen who had started to arrive in larger numbers. National attention resulted in 1872 when Pres. Ulysses S. Grant visited George Pullman (of Pullman railroad car fame) at his nearby island home, Castle Rest. By *c.* 1873, the village boasted two deluxe hotels, several thriving businesses, and a brisk summer tourist trade. The community benefited enormously through catering to the needs of its visitors, its size and services expanding accordingly. By this time, the area had also become much more easily accessible due to more frequent steamship service, as well as railroad access in nearby Clayton.

In 1845, Ezeriah Walton, a local lumber trader, purchased in company with one Chesterfield Pearson, the north half of Well's Island (now Wellesley Island), as well as all the smaller islands in the American Channel from Clayton to Morristown. Upon his death in 1855, the firm of Cornwall & Walton bought them from his estate for purposes of logging. Once coal began to replace wood, *c.* 1860, the firm began to sell the islands off at reasonable prices, encouraging the building of summer cottages upon them. This proved very successful, and their development created yet more opportunity in the village.

The tour-boat business, an important part of our tourist-driven economy, was born in 1874, when Capt. Elisha Visger began giving tours through the islands in his small steamer, the *Signet*. The Alexandria Bay Steamboat Company was organized in 1887 and built the steamer *New Island Wanderer*, further accommodating the growing demand for island tours. By the turn of the century, a golden age had developed, attended by the appropriate splendor and extravagance that gave the period its name. However, the Great Depression brought this grand period to somewhat of a halt in the 1930s. After the nation's recovery, the community stabilized into the seasonal resort that it remains to this day.

The tourist season is essential, but short, from Memorial Day to Labor Day. Beneath the celebrity of being a favorite summer destination lies a village rich in the special qualities found in the increasingly rare American small-town community. The final chapter of this book celebrates our continuing sense of community and pays tribute, by picturing but a few, to all those who have worked so diligently through the years to make the village all that it is.

This welcome sign, known as the arch, graces the entrance to the village at the intersection of Church and Otter Streets. An article in the *Thousand Islands Sun* stated that it was illuminated for the first time during the week of September 4, 1924. It still greets visitors upon their arrival.

One

THE EARLY YEARS

A very early view, before 1900, depicts one of the two main intersections on James Street, the main thoroughfare of downtown. Both the house at the corner of James and Market Streets and the Bailey Block, visible just beyond it, are still standing and in use.

The buildings housing these two businesses and the post office are still located on lower James Street in the commercial heart of the village. The date recorded at the top of the Bailey Block building, on the left, indicates 1896 to have been the building's date of origin. The second-story porch no longer exists.

Not an unusual combination for the times, this retail venue dealt in furniture and caskets, serving the community as its only funeral home. Pictured are Ernest Reynolds (left), Charles Haas (center), and Norris Houghton. In 1920, Charles Giltz became proprietor, and the Giltz Funeral Home is still in operation today. This picture is dated 1907.

Seen in this vintage photograph is a typical produce store of the late 1800s. David D. Long maintained grocery stores during this period in both Oswego and Alexandria Bay.

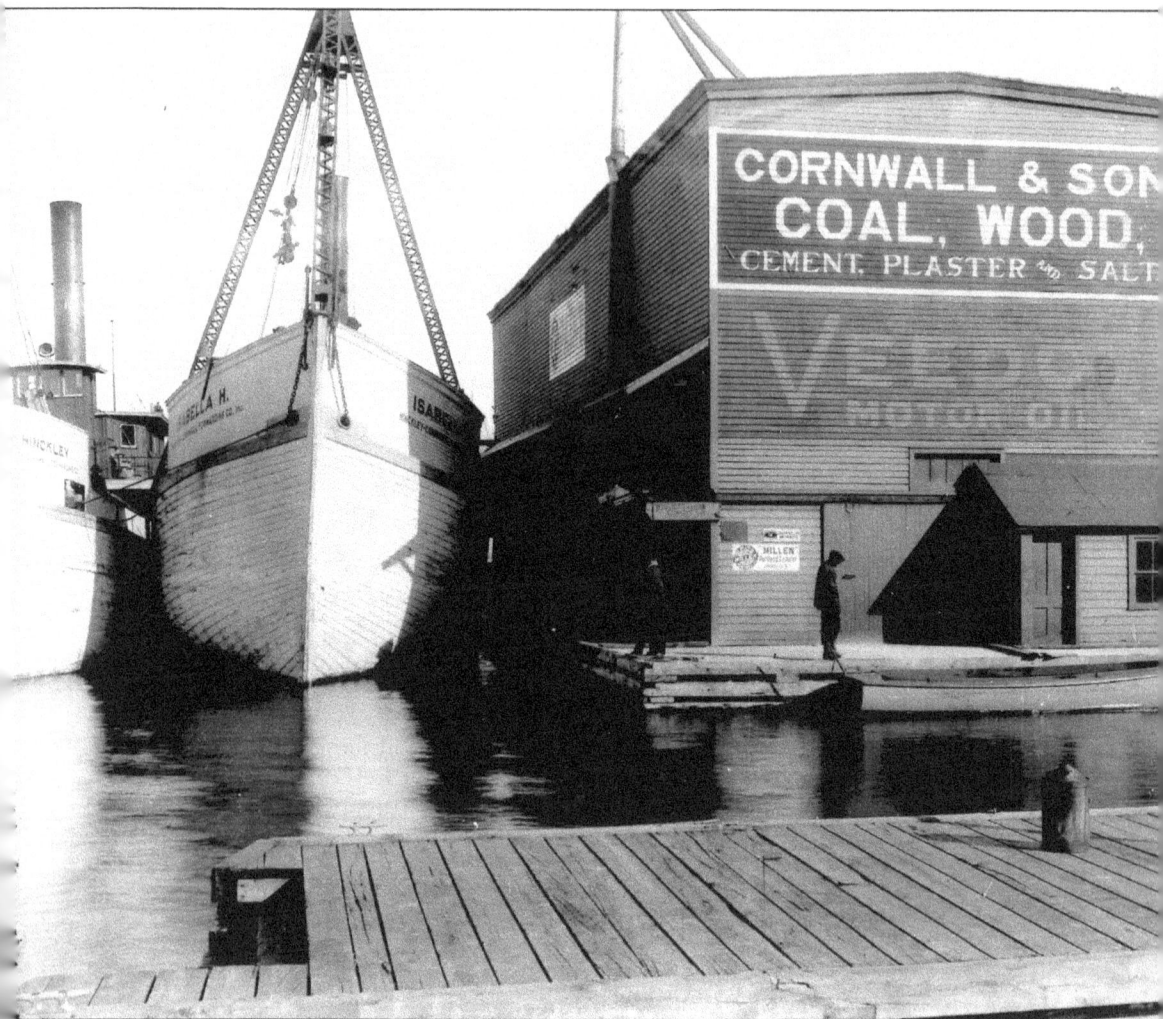

Not only did the industrious Cornwall family maintain a retail store, but one of Andrew Cornwall's four sons also began this lumber and coal supply, located on the Lower Bay.

Cornwall Brothers was established in 1846 by Andrew Cornwall and L. A. Walton under the firm name of L. A. Walton & Company, later becoming Cornwall & Walton. In 1877, under the direction of Cornwall's four sons, it became Cornwall Brothers. Originally, its main business consisted of cutting and buying, and shipping to Montreal and Quebec, square timber and vessel spars. Having also purchased all islands between Clayton and Morristown, and by selling them off at a nominal fee, they were also instrumental in the early surge of development of the islands as a summer resort.

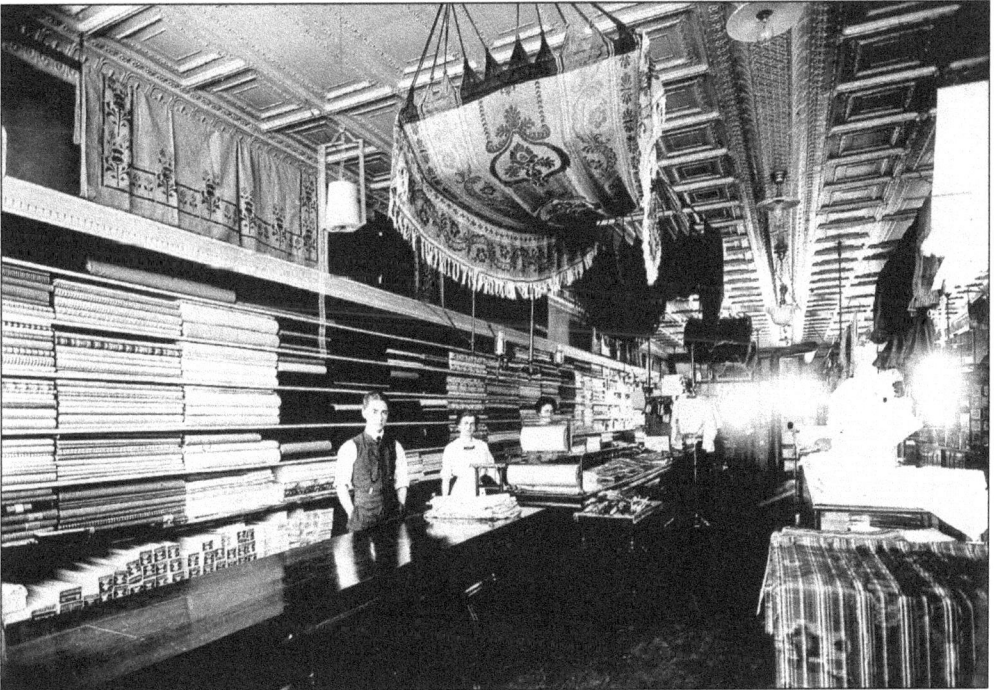

As witnessed in this 1914 photograph, the Cornwall Brothers emporium offered an array of wares. Pictured are store clerks Albert Hartman (left), May Springer (center), and an unidentified employee.

CORNWALL BROTHERS'
GENERAL TICKET AGENTS,

Alexandria Bay, Jefferson County, N. Y.

Tickets for Quebec, Ha-Ha Bay, Gulf Ports, Halifax, Portland, Boston, White Mountains, Lake Champlain, Lake George, Saratoga, New York, and all points East and West, sold at

LOWEST EXCURSION RATES.

Secure your tickets before taking the Steamers and save the difference between Local and Excursion Rates. Baggage checked to all points. Also dealers in

DOMESTIC AND FANCY DRY GOODS,
NOTIONS, CARPETS, HATS, CAPS, CLOTHING, BOOTS AND SHOES,

Groceries, Fishing Tackle,

Hardware, Crockery, Paints, Oils, Etc.

They pay CASH for all their purchases, thereby getting the Benefit of all Discounts, which enables them to sell goods cheap. They have also a

❧CUSTOM TAILORING DEPARTMENT,❧

In charge of one of the *best* and most *experienced* cutters in the country.

CAMP AND ISLAND SUPPLIES
—AND—

FANCY GROCERIES

They make a specialty.

They employ experienced and courteous salesmen who do not consider it trouble to show goods. All are cordially invited to call and see them.

ALEXANDRIA BAY, JUNE, 1884.

A further testament to the Cornwalls' "soup to nuts" involvement in every facet of commerce is apparent in this bulletin advertising their travel agency and fine grocery offerings.

This 1909 interior view of the post office suggests that by this time the office had moved from James Street to Hopewell Lodge No. 854, the International Order of Odd Fellows building on Market Street, erected in 1907. Elbert E. Makepeace (right) was postmaster from 1899 to 1913. George Russell (left) was assistant postmaster and a post office employee for 22 years.

This view of James Street, looking toward the Lower Bay, provides the backdrop for a most impressive lineup of early automobiles in 1914. This was and still is the hub of downtown activity in the bay.

The St. Lawrence International Electric Railroad and Land Company introduced trolley service between Redwood and Alexandria Bay, making its inaugural run on the evening of August 17, 1902. The line was seven and a half miles in length and initially consisted of three cars, two open and one closed. Pictured here is the enclosed passenger car, which was 44 feet long. This car also accommodated baggage service.

The two open passenger cars were each outfitted with 15 benches and were powered by four engines of 37 horsepower each. Upon arrival in Redwood, one could make connections with Pullman service to New York City and Boston.

This building on Otter Street served as the carbarn for the trolley company. After the line ceased operation, it became a storehouse. Ownership has changed hands several times. Owners have included the Niagara Mohawk Power Corporation, Edgewood Resort, and currently, Aqua Mania, a boat-rental and sales concern located on Otter Creek.

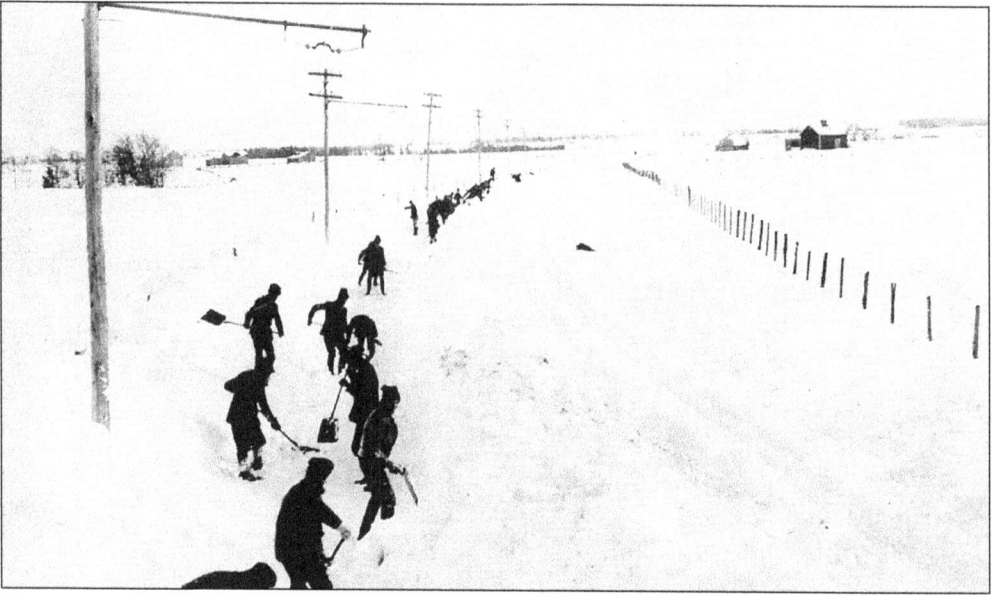

These men have their work cut out for them in the clearing of the trolley tracks after a substantial snow accumulation in the early 1900s.

A wintertime trolley occupant might, for seven and a half miles, have nothing more than a continuous wall of snow on both sides of the coach as his or her view.

18

After several years of operation, service deteriorated and complaints became frequent. By c. 1916, the advent of private automobile and bus travel had made a significant enough impact that the trolley finally discontinued operations.

The original edifice of the 1000 Islands opera house stood behind the Masonic temple on James Street. Before demolition, it had become the village convention hall.

In the late 1800s existed a local acting troupe, Ye Young Cadets, seen posing at a performance of *A Cadet's Picnic* on November 6, 1889. The drummer boy is Capt. George Comstock, of a locally prominent family.

This home at the corner of James and Market Streets (seen previously in a very early postcard), was originally the J. W. Fuller family homestead. Later, Lois Thomson, née Fuller, resided there.

This Thomson family portrait was taken at the Crossman Street residence of Arthur Thomson. Seen here are the following: (front row) little Will Mitchell, an unidentified woman, and the family pet; (middle row, seated) William H. Thomson, Sarah Carter Thomson (William H. Thomson's wife), and Sally Thomson Foss; (back row) Arthur Thomson, Lucien Mitchell, Curry Thomson Mitchell, Josephine Walton, Flora Thomson, and Sadie Walton.

This group portrait of Alexandria Bay's young elite was taken in July 1898. From left to right are the following: (front row) Clarence Thomson, Henry Leyare, Linnie Houghton, and Fuller Cornwall; (middle row) Lorine Watson, Mame Hayes, Norris Houghton, Belle Cline, and Bess Cornwall; (back row) Clarence Kepler, Lillian Houghton, and Andrew Thomson.

This family group enjoys a day's outing with their naphtha launch *Spry*. Among them are James Albert Parker and Kate Dingman Parker (in the far left foreground) and Jane Porter Dingman and John Dingman (holding baby Captola and standing to the far right). These surnames continue in prominence today.

This and the preceding photograph reveal typical river sojourns during the late 19th and early 20th centuries. Large groups would routinely make daylong excursions that included shore dinners, music, and games. The tradition is quietly carried on by many villagers today, who utilize their own camps and river homes or facilities now available at state parks on various islands.

The Alexandria Bay High School football team and its supporters pose for a group shot in 1900. Identified are Walter Houghton (1), George Chane (4), Charlie Stine (5), Eddie Deer (6), Frank Swan (8), Pete Leonard (10), Frank Whalen (11), Billy Wall (13), Edie Campbell (14), Rupert Houghton (15), Walter Visger Jr. (17), Guy Leonard (18), Clay Kepler (19), Frank Combs (20), Will Visger (21), John George (22), Harry Brownhill (23), Newell Service (25), Gus Rogers (26), Claude VanDresar (27), Edith Hoadley (28), Ida Barker (29), John Cornwall (30), Leon Cornwall (31), Herbert West (32), Harold West (33), Lew Hartman (35), Bert Howe (36), and Ray Cornwall.

These dapper gentlemen pose for Duncan McIntyre (the village photographer, along with A. C. McIntyre, before 1900) along the stone steps at the Crossman House. Seated are, from left to right, George De Zel, M. Henry, Jim Brophey, H. C. Kepler, George Wall, Joe David, and Ryley Perry (front). Standing are, from left to right, Billy Wall, Eddie Campbell, Jack Thebault, Ben ?, Raymond Cornwall, and Frank Capron.

This hose brigade demonstration is likely during a firemen's convention, an event that has been hosted by the local fire department many times for over 100 years.

The New Carlton Hotel stood for many years on the corner of James and Church Streets. These firefighters were not able to save the building from this conflagration in 1939, and it went down in flames.

The Combined Boat Tours resulted from a consolidation of a number of independent operators in 1927. The operation later became Uncle Sam Boat Tours, which continues at this location today.

The notation on the reverse of this photograph identifies these sophisticated young men only as members of "Tammany O" and as having just shared Christmas dinner.

The Angler's Association met often at the Crossman House. In addition to being avid fishermen, they were also dedicated to the protection and propagating of game fish. They maintained fisheries that stocked the St. Lawrence with fry.

This home and adjoining shop at 43 Church Street are seen here prior to c. 1925, when the business became Sam Guerrieri's clothing store. Tony Folino became its occupant in 1934 and operated Folino's shoe store at this location for 65 years.

The Crossman House kept a group of donkeys in the donkey pasture for the entertainment of guests. Astride one sits a very young Elof Hansson, later to become a stonecutter and gardener in the village.

A portion of the Lower Bay and the Main Channel is dotted with Cornwall Brothers (foreground), the Marsden House (behind Cornwall), and the Crossman House (right center).

Two

HOTELS AND
LANDMARKS

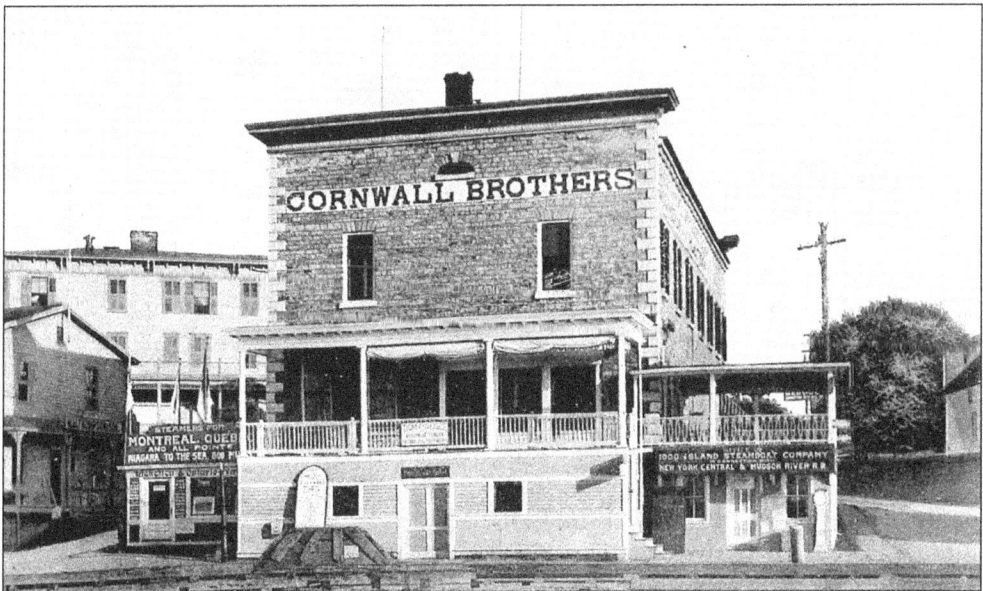

The *Jefferson County Historical Review of 1884* described Cornwall Brothers as a mercantile "carrying the largest line of general merchandise to be found in this section." Stock consisted of "camp and island supplies . . . a specialty, dry goods, notions, hats and caps, boots and shoes, groceries, crockery, hardware, clothing, etc., etc." The second floor was devoted expressly to custom tailoring, with a bountiful selection of fabrics from which to choose. To all this was added a general ticket agency.

The Crossman House, on lower James Street, was Alexandria Bay's first deluxe hotel, opening its doors in 1872. The need for such accommodation arose after the region gained prominence through a visit by Pres. Ulysses S. Grant. After nearly a century of first-class hospitality, the building was finally deemed a safety hazard and razed in 1962.

Following the successful opening of the Crossman House, the nearby Thousand Island House was completed in 1873 under the command of Col. O. G. Staples, at a cost of $100,000. It was located on the waterfront property now occupied by River Hospital. The concrete dock and lowest stone wall still exist.

The Marsden House, located opposite the Cornwall Brothers store on the waterfront, finally went the way of all such Victorian edifices in the region. It was razed in the 1960s after a devastating fire. Today, only a vacant lot remains where it once reigned in modest dignity.

Although the resort-hotel clientele consisted mainly of Americans, the employees appear to be of many nations. Here, a hotel kitchen staff pauses for a group portrait.

This Edgewood candid was taken c. 1903. The resort began in 1886, when J. M. Curtiss of Cleveland, Ohio, erected a three-story hotel, followed by the building of another cottage for hotel overflow. It still exists and bears the name of its founder. Although it has had numerous owners over the years, Edgewood has endured and remains in operation.

Following the discontinuation of the trolley, bus lines served to fulfill public transportation needs. The first service between Alexandria Bay and Watertown commenced in 1922. In 1936, Murray Taitt, then driving for Greyhound, took over the Alexandria Bay route. Here, in 1937, Murray stands in front of the New St. Lawrence Hotel, at James and Church Streets, next to his REO Speed Wagon deluxe bus. It held 21 passengers and included the Canadian mainland, as well as Watertown, on its route.

Dec. 29, 1922

The Thousand Islands Country Club, Wellesley Island, is located across the river from Alexandria Bay. It is seen here under construction in 1922, and the following photograph shows the club in the late 1920s.

Built as a private club, the Thousand Islands Country Club was for many years part of the E. J. Noble estate.

Not all tourists were obliged to stay only in the grand hotels along the waterfront. Less fancy but perfectly attractive accommodations were available in rooming houses like this one, operated initially as such by Mrs. Henry Hartman, later by C. B. and Harriet LaLonde Tidd, and finally by the R. Gareth Service family through the early 1960s. It was located at 21 Church Street, currently the site of a restaurant.

Another lovely tourist accommodation, the Hill Crest, on Walton Street, offered quarters a little removed from the downtown area.

A third, equally pleasant accommodation existed at this residence on Avery Avenue, just past the arch, off Church Street. The house still stands.

Construction of Boldt Castle on Heart Island, opposite Alexandria Bay and across the main channel of the St. Lawrence, began in 1900. Granite excavated on Oak Island 10 miles downriver was utilized in its construction. In 1904, upon receiving word of the untimely death of his beloved wife, Louise, George Boldt ceased all work. For years his intended valentine (the island was blasted into the shape of a heart) sat abandoned and in disrepair. The island is now owned by the Thousand Islands Bridge Authority, and ongoing renovation of the castle, outbuildings, and grounds has made it the premier tourist destination of the region.

George C. Boldt was born on the Prussian island of Rugen, in the Baltic Sea, in 1851. In 1864, he immigrated to America as a near-penniless youth of 13. Ambitious and optimistic, he diligently built a career as hotelier and entrepreneur, quickly rising to great heights financially. He and his bride, Louise, visited the Thousand Islands for the first time c. 1895. By the time of his death in 1916, he held positions in the business world as president of the Waldorf-Astoria hotel company; proprietor of the Belleview-Stratford Hotel in Philadelphia; director of the Commonwealth Trust Company, the Lincoln Trust Company, and the North British and Mercantile Insurance Company of London and Edinburgh; and director of the Hotel Association of New York City, to name a few. This photograph was taken the year he died, 1916.

George Boldt contributed generously to the betterment of Alexandria Bay, granting funds, as well as gifts (in this case, books), to village institutions.

Alster Tower, at water's edge, was the first of the planned 11 structures to be erected on Heart Island and became the Boldts' summer home during construction of the castle. Its design was inspired by a castle on the Rhine, and it contained a bowling alley, ballroom, and guest suites on the upper floors. Plans for a library, billiard room, café, and other facilities were never completed in Boldt's time.

The powerhouse with a clock tower was fashioned after a medieval tower and was to contain not only a generating plant, but also the rooms to lodge its engineers and mechanics.

The Arch of Triumph, at the western end of the island, is a water gate through which one passes into a lagoon surrounding a good portion of the island. The original lagoon was over 500 feet long and was intended to serve as a swan pond. The three deer atop the arch were in the original plans but only recently realized and installed by the Thousand Island Bridge Authority.

This beautiful shell fountain had, like the castle itself, fallen into disrepair but has now been restored to its original condition. It sits on the Alexandria Bay side and at the east end of the island.

The main entrance hall is now renovated to its original intended condition.

After the main dining room was renovated, it was refurbished with period furniture and accoutrements appropriate to the period.

The grand staircase, leading from the main entrance hall to the second floor, has recently been renovated. Some 10,000 pounds of white Georgian marble were utilized in the process.

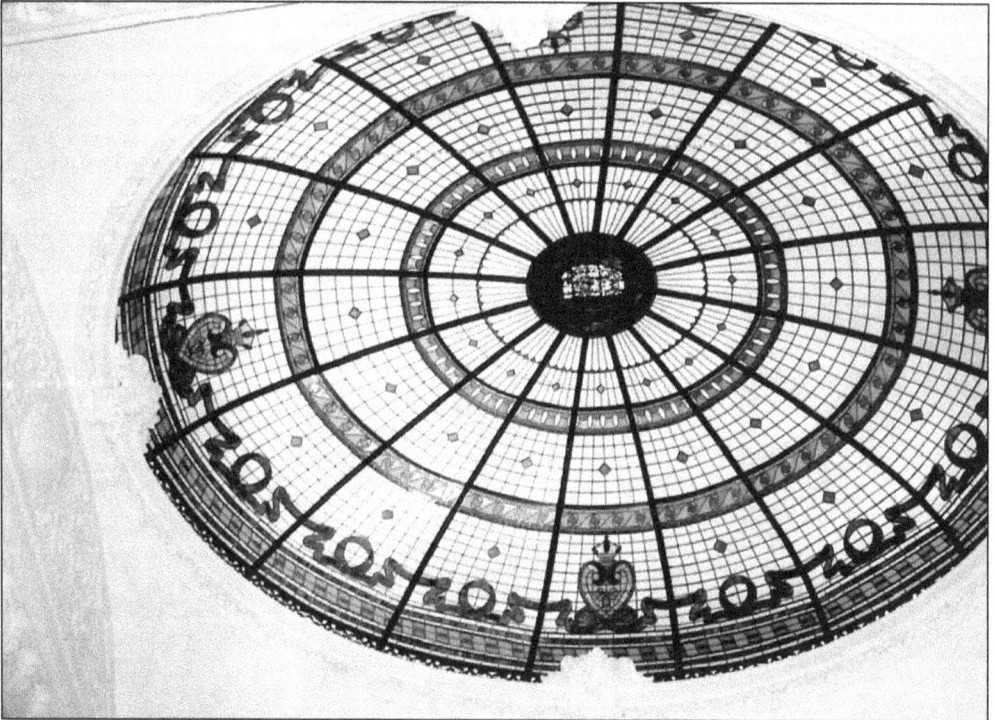

This spectacular stained-glass dome was a part of the original plan and installed in 2000 as part of the ongoing renovation. It contains over 6,000 individual pieces of stained glass and over one mile of lead caming.

The architectural firm of Hewitt, Stephens and Paist of Philadelphia was engaged by Boldt with the admonition that expense was of no concern. Although the firm provided all of the drawings, the inspiration for them came entirely from the Boldts. Detail tended toward the intricate.

This group of workers, employed by George Boldt, is seen during a break on the back farm, located on Wellesley Island. This farm's poultry and produce were shipped to Boldt's hotels in Philadelphia and New York. Seen here are, from left to right, two unidentified Italian immigrants, Charlie Hogan, Gordon Wilber, William Plimpton, Ted Reynolds, Emerson ?, Ed Reynolds, Charles Snyder, and "Dug" Raye.

The Boldts' three yachts and houseboat were accommodated in this yacht house, directly across from the castle, on Wellesley Island. The boat slips measure 128 feet, and the building itself is 64 feet in height. It housed a shop to build race boats, as well as living quarters for crew and staff. The yacht house has undergone major renovations and is now open to the public, displaying an array of antique wooden boats, some from the original Boldt fleet.

The *Presto*, built by yacht builder C. D. Mosher in 1903, was sold two years later by Boldt to Nathan Strauss of Cherry Island. It was 75 feet long with a 9.5-foot beam. Here, a group of Boldt staff has assembled with Mosher for an inspection of the craft.

One of the Boldt yachts, the *Louise*, and a smaller launch sit at rest, docked at Wellesley Island.

The Thousand Islands Bridge System connects the U.S. mainland to Canada. This first of four spans, the American span is located at Collins Landing, near Alexandria Bay, and extends to Wellesley Island. This suspension bridge main span measures 800 feet and provides clearance of 150 feet above the water.

From groundbreaking in May 1937 to completion in 1938, the bridge system took just 16 months to complete. The American span is pictured during initial stages of deck paving in 1938.

Construction continued throughout the winter months, no doubt a daunting task considering North Country winters.

The surfacing of the American span was near completion in this photograph.

The first car in the dedication ceremonies motorcade was that of Pres. Franklin D. Roosevelt.

With President Roosevelt was Canadian Prime Minister Mackenzie King. Here, the two preside over the ribbon-cutting ceremonies, which attracted more than 25,000 people to the international border.

This early panorama of the Alexandria Bay waterfront depicts the premier hotels in business and their locations relative to one another c. 1900. The Crossman House is on the left, the Marsden House (behind Cornwall Brothers) is in the center, and the Thousand Island House stands on the right.

Three

CHURCHES
AND SCHOOLS

One early county record states that the first schoolhouse in Alexandria Bay consisted of a log cabin built in 1821 on the current site of the Reformed church. Conflicting data from another county document indicates that a rent of 75¢ a month was paid to Abel Root for rental of a room to serve as the school as of 1826. A contribution of half a cord of wood was required of each student as tuition. By 1886, spatial restraints necessitated the construction of this large wooden building, which sat across from the Methodist church, on the corner of Church and Rock Streets. The photograph is dated *c.* 1898.

The brick addition seen on the left was added to the original wooden structure in 1903, dating this class portrait sometime shortly after its completion.

This third-grade class of 1912–1913 has students with surnames recognizable today in the area. Included in the photograph are the following: (first row) Glenn Furnace, Clifford Dobbins, Helen Haas Gormley, Thelma Simmons Root, Maxine Lilly Regan, Dodie Jones, Madyln Patience, Genevieve Hunt, Elizabeth Houghton, Frances Collins, Lucile Truesdell, and ? Estes; (second row) Newell Paige, Neil Regan, ? Jobson, Luke Roy, James Rae, Helen Rogers, Dorothy Miller Scott, Flora Rogers Smalling, and Geraldine Kavanaugh; (third row) John Dobbins, Wesley Queal, Clifford Kavanaugh, Ralph Willix, Virgil Hoffman, Andrew LaFirst, Orrin Davis, Rena Trickey Ely, Earl Wagoner, and Geraldine Wilson; (fourth row) Laura Sturdevant (schoolmistress).

Construction of the school currently in use was begun in May 1927, and the building was dedicated on August 31, 1928. The total cost was $325,000. It boasts an auditorium seating 500, as well as a gymnasium and an addition of grade-school classrooms built over the intervening years.

Alexandria Central School athletes attended their annual awards banquet in 1950. An esteemed coach of many years, George Brown is in the center of the back row in a white shirt and tie.

Construction of the Reformed Protestant Dutch Church (now the Reformed Church of the 1000 Islands) was spearheaded by summer visitor Rev. George W. Bethune, and the church opened its doors for worship on May 25, 1851. The original 35- by 55-foot structure, with a 60-foot-high clock tower, was able to accommodate 350 to 400 people. According to L. H. Everts & Company's *History of Jefferson County of 1878*, it was completed at a cost of $2,822, the clock tower bell costing $170.

The parish of St. Cyril's Catholic Church was formed *c.* 1881, originally under the name St. Joseph's; at first, Father Manning of the Redwood parish said Sunday mass in private homes or the schoolhouse. This original church and its rectory were built *c.* 1903 on the Houghton property at the corner of Crossman and Rockwell Streets.

A growing parish and the influx of summer tourists proved the old church inadequate. The cornerstone for this beautiful granite structure was laid on June 18, 1922, and the church was dedicated upon completion in 1925. After being purchased from the Bachman family, their home, built in 1903 (part of which is visible here), became the church rectory.

The cornerstone for the Episcopal Church of St. Lawrence was laid on October 8, 1887, and the building was completed by 1891. The contractor was Albert Bachman of this village. The building's existence is owed to a number of summer islanders who gave generously to its construction fund. It features handsome hardwood wainscoting throughout, as well as a magnificent stained-glass window.

The First Methodist Episcopal Church (now the United Methodist Church) of Alexandria Bay, according to the 1890 Child's Gazetteer, was built at a cost of $6,500 and would accommodate 280 worshipers. It was erected in 1875, and its first pastor was Rev. William M. Holbrook.

58

The interior of the Dutch Reformed church was lavishly decorated for the wedding ceremony of Simon J. Vroman and Lillian Houghton, which took place on September 16, 1908.

An early church-school group gathered for a portrait outside the Methodist church on Church Street. From the plethora of fancy bonnets, one might conclude it was Easter.

The ubiquitous St. Lawrence skiff was regularly utilized for work and for play in the late 1800s and early 1900s. This camping party made obvious good use of theirs.

Four

A BOAT CULTURE

The classic St. Lawrence rowing skiff is among the narrower, yet sturdy, round-bottom rowboats. Its prevalence resulted from the ever burgeoning need of fishing guides and sportsmen who tended the recreational needs of an affluent summer population from the grand hotels. A product of boatbuilders all along the river, the *Champion* was designed and built by A. E. Furness of Bethune Street, on the Upper Bay.

Seen here is a gang of Alexandria Bay fellows on a day's outing. They are, from left to right, as follows: (seated) Charles White, unidentified, John Kellett, C. U. Putnam, and Bert DeYoung; (standing) Delbert Haas, John T. DeLaney, F. Howard Scott, Fred Wicks, two unidentified men, and Claude Ellis. Seated on the cabin roof in the front is Ross Visger, and the man on the roof in the back is unidentified. Fuller Cornwall is seated on the far left, in the back.

The palace steamer *St. Lawrence*, the flagship of the Folger Brothers Steamship Company "White Squadron," had a capacity of 900 passengers. It made regular tours, called scenic rambles, through the islands and offered an on-deck musical trio as accompaniment to the trip. With Boldt Castle in the background, this photograph dates from *c.* 1900, possibly a little later.

Traffic at the Cornwall Brothers dock was brisk. As the *St. Lawrence* departs, another steamship approaches to take its place.

The *Captain Visger* was owned and operated by the son of Capt. E. W. Visger, a pioneer tour boat navigator and guide. It was 90 feet in length with a 13.5-foot beam and had a capacity of 110 passengers. It also specialized in searchlight tours after dusk. Bonnie Castle is seen in the background.

This very familiar scene is repeated today, many times every day, up and down the St. Lawrence River, all summer long. Tourism was and remains our principal industry.

The *Captain Visger* is shown as it approached a dock by the Thousand Island House, where excursionists could disembark.

Just below the Thousand Island House, adjacent to Cornwall Brothers, passengers gathered to catch a Combined Boat Tours launch for a sightseeing tour. Note the change in boat by the 1920s, as gasoline engines took over and boats became smaller and more streamlined.

The *Sis V* joined the growing fleet of tour boats plying the waters around Alexandria Bay in the summer of 1929. It had been built locally at Hutchinson's Boat Works. Its new owner, J. P. Wagoner, captained his own ship.

Another beautiful craft of slightly earlier style and vintage than the *Sis V* sits at Edgewood Point in front of two guest homes owned and operated by Fred Knight. The homes later became part of Edgewood Resort and are currently private residences.

Yet another beautiful passenger boat is seen here, this one varnished and sporting ornate scroll decoration at the bow. Note the early braided-rope bumpers atop the deck.

Luxurious boat limousines like this one were a conspicuous sight on the river up through the 1950s and 1960s. Although greatly diminished in number, these marvelous craft are still occasionally seen on the river.

The *Buzz*, built by Louis Kenyon, has been in the Clark family of Comfort Island for nearly a century. Here, Mancel T. Clark, then about age 18, is seen running his craft just off the tip of Comfort Island. Comfort's large boathouse looms in the background.

A chauffeur drives his passengers down the main channel in the *Swiftwater*. The residence of the same name is just beyond the Thousand Islands Bridge on Wellesley Island. This boat was owned by the original owner of that estate.

Another boat captain, in proper regalia, sits affront Boldt Castle for his photo opportunity. The boat is a 1930s 22-foot Chris-Craft. The captain is unidentified.

The legend on the reverse of this 1920s photograph indicates that it was not fish that were being transported across the United States–Canadian border in this boat during Prohibition.

The speedboat *Miss England* was designed for racing and was often in pursuit of the coveted gold cup—hence, the moniker "gold cup races." For 9 of the first 11 years, the cup was won by 1000 Islands contenders from one of the following: the Thousand Islands Yacht Club, the Chippewa Bay Yacht Club, or the Frontenac Yacht Club.

The *Miss Toronto* was another frequent contender. The first of the American Power Boat Association (APBA) Gold Cup races was held on the Hudson River in June 1904 over a 32-mile course. The winning speed of 23.16 miles per hour, clocked by the 40-foot *Standard*, was considered amazing at the time.

The seventh race, which took place in August 1909, was held here on the Thousand Islands Yacht Club course and won by one of its own, the *Dixie II*, owned by Frederick K. Burham of New York City.

These two racers, Jack Bickell (left) and J. G. Ericson, owned and piloted the *Miss Toronto*. Life preservers were quite basic in the early 1900s.

SECOND ANNUAL

Thousand Islands

(IN JEFFERSON & ST. LAWRENCE COUNTIES, NEW YORK STATE)

INTERNATIONAL
STOCK OUTBOARD MARATHON

$5,000.⁰⁰ MERCHANDISE PRIZES!

SUNDAY, JUNE 12, 1955

St. Lawrence River

A.P.B.A.
Sanctioned

Sponsored By

The Chambers of Commerce of
Alexandria Bay, N.Y.

Brockville, Ont.

Clayton, N.Y.

Ogdensburg, N.Y.

Watertown, N.Y.

For many years, Alexandria Bay hosted the annual International Stock Outboard Marathon in front of the village on the main channel. Shown is the entry form from the 1955 event.

Hunter Grimes II was a regular contender and frequent winner of the outboard competition. Here, Grimes flies through the air with the greatest of ease. His son, Hunter Grimes III, has followed his father's lead and continues to compete around the country today.

An entirely different endeavor from the building of race and pleasure craft existed locally as well. Hutchinson's Boat Works had contracts in both world wars to build boats for the U.S. Navy. In World War I, they built wooden "lighters."

During World War II, the boats built by Hutchinson's for the navy were 75-foot YP boats, as seen in this shot. Information pertaining to the boats' construction was considered confidential, and Keep Out signage said as much.

A regular sight in early spring was the *Sampson*, a workhorse efficient in breaking up the ice in the bays. It was the first all-steel-hull boat built by Glenn Furness of Bethune Street and was later owned by Hutchinson's Boat Works. Here, it is seen at work in the Upper Bay.

The Alexandria Bay Fire Department has maintained for years a fireboat to service the islands. In this and in the following photograph, two different craft that have served that function are pictured.

Regular testing of the equipment assured against malfunction in an emergency.

These builders pause for a break during final stages of construction of their fireboat. They are, from left to right, Theron Hartman, Glenn Wilson, Jarvis VanBrocklin, Louis Evans, William Strough, Fred Dobbins, William Plimpton, and Wallace Solar.

Rev. James L. Meehan is seen bestowing a prayer upon the *Donald H. Gamble*, the rescue squad craft, during the annual blessing of the fleet. This is an annual Alexandria Bay tradition, and all are welcome to have their craft blessed.

The St. Lawrence Seaway is a vital transportation route for the shipment of goods to points west and attracts tankers from virtually every country. Here, the *Orsala*, out of Dubrovnik, Croatia, heads downriver after passing through from the Great Lakes. From its height out of water, it is clear that the ship has already unloaded its cargo.

Snow and ice do not deter the intrepid *Thousand Islander*. Here, Junior Dingman (at the throttle) and Trey Vars enjoyed an airboat ride in 1969.

A larger iceboat, with an airplane engine rigged in the rear, makes its way down the channel in open water.

Accidents have happened on the shipping channel; fortunately, they do not happen often. Here, the *Jean Parisien* misjudged and ended up on a shoal sometime in the 1980s.

Another tragic boat-related event is seen here, at the Thurston Ship Yard fire on May 12, 1918. Destroyed were, among others, the yacht *Klotawah* and a ferry boat (foreground), still under construction at the time of fire.

This beautiful 1930s, wooden, Garwood inboard runabout has become, if not extinct, a rare breed of boat among the usual recreational craft of today, most of which are constructed from fiberglass and plastics.

Five

AMONG THE ISLANDS

For a day's idyllic outing among the Thousand Islands, it was common for a steam yacht to tow rowing skiffs to a designated location, tie up, and have the guests disembark for the smaller craft, handy for exploring in shallow water.

The serene beauty of the view from the Alexandria Bay waterfront prevails regardless of season.

Casa Blanca, on Cherry Island, was built c. 1895 by the owner of a large sugar plantation in Cuba, a woman with the surname Marx. Her daughter sold the property c. 1960 to Al and Edith Amsterdam, in whose family the property remains. The house is entirely furnished with pieces appropriate to the date of its construction and features a magnificent staircase graced, at the second-floor landing, with a large and intricate stained-glass window.

Hopewell Hall was originally the summer home of W. C. Browning of New York City. It featured extensively landscaped gardens throughout the grounds. It later became home to Clover Boldt, the granddaughter of George Boldt. Upon her death, the property was sold to the current residents, who have made extensive renovations and improvements in recent years.

The palatial summer cottage called Ingleside, on Cherry Island, was one of two twin houses. Ingleside was built by Abraham Abraham. The house beside it, Belora (which is no longer in existence), was built by Abraham's business partner, Nathan Strauss. Together, they owned Abraham & Strauss department stores of New York City. Abraham's yacht, the *Rose*, is dockside.

One of Abraham's steam yachts, the *Wana*, sits moored to docks on the back side of his home, Ingleside, on Cherry Island.

Abraham Abraham, builder and first resident of Ingleside on Cherry Island, is pictured here with grandchildren under the portico of his island home.

The Birches, on Wellesley Island, was another beautiful villa of the Boldt estates.

Oak Lodge, also on Wellesley Island, was built in 1900 by the recently widowed Louise Schultz to serve as a getaway for her large family. It boasts 16 bedrooms and 22 rooms altogether. It changed proprietors in 1926, when it was sold to the Kincaid family. It remains the homestead of Kincaid descendants today.

Construction of this house on Comfort Island was begun in 1882, and the house was first occupied in 1883. A. E. Clark of Chicago, along with his wife, Sarah, and three sons, made the annual trek by train to summer here. It has remained in the Clark family since it was built.

The Thousand Islands Yacht Club was located on Welcome Island. Along with myriad other activities, it sponsored boat races and hosted the gold cup. It was torn down many years ago, and in its place is now a private residence.

The interior of the Thousand Islands Yacht Club is seen decorated in preparation for its inaugural festivities in the summer of 1895.

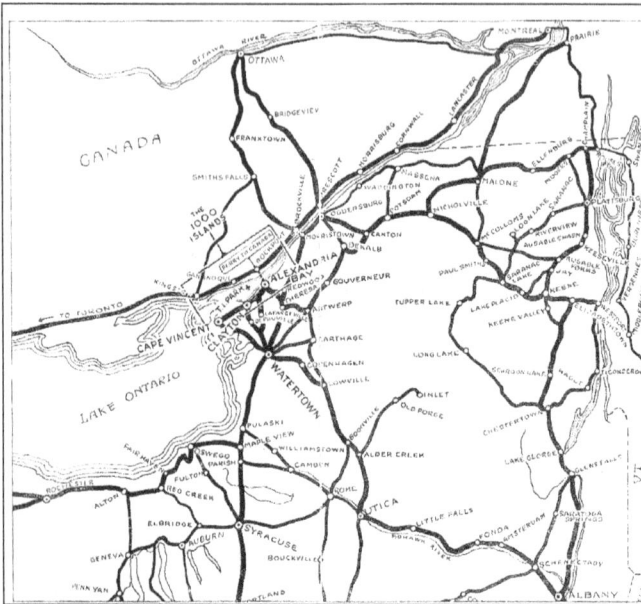

This brochure for Hutchinson's Ferry, whose ferries ran between Alexandria Bay and the Canadian village of Rockport, gives a reasonable overview of the position of the village relative to its neighboring towns along the river.

There were a number of ferry companies making connections between the American and Canadian shores up and down the river. Here are two of the Hutchinson's Ferry fleet. The last of the lines providing this service runs from Cape Vincent, 30 miles upriver, on the American side.

90

Six

EVENTS AND ATTRACTIONS

Miniature golf was a favorite pastime in the summer months, and there were several courses available. Pictured is the North Star, which was located on the grounds now occupied by the North Star Motel and restaurant just past the arch, on Route 12.

This anonymous golfer prepares his swing. Golf has endured as a popular sport in Alexandria Bay, and there are several courses in the vicinity of the village today.

THE AUTOMOBILE RACING
CLUB OF AMERICA

Official Program

PRICE—10c

Alexandria Bay
"Round The Houses" Road Race
Alexandria Bay, N. Y.
AUGUST 7, 1937

This official program announces the popular racing event of the 1930s and 1940s, the Automobile Racing Club of America's Round the Houses Race. Inside were entry lists, lap sheets, and score cards, as well as a warning that races were "dangerous and spectators attending do so entirely at their own risk."

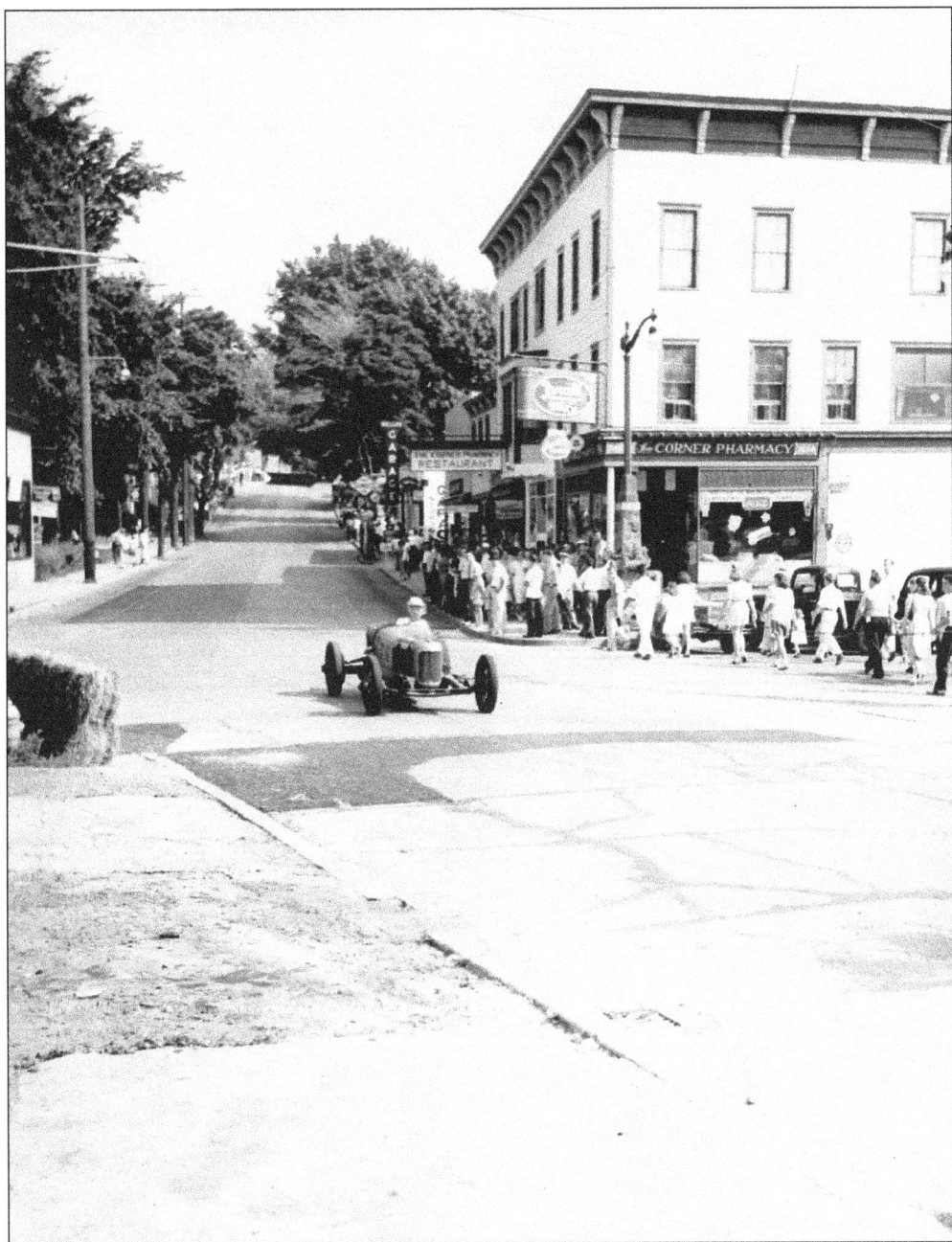

In a 1939 race, this contender crosses the intersection of Church and James Streets, passing the Hartman Block, then home to Harold Edick's corner pharmacy.

During the 1950s, stock-car racing was a popular sport at the Edgewood Park speedway. Dick Warner stands next to his *Hot Tomato*. A 1957 *Watertown Times* article reported that "turning in one of the best performances seen here this summer, Dick Warner, local stock car race driver carried away championship honors in the 50-lap Labor Day Race that was held at the Edgewood Park speedway on Monday afternoon."

Avid race fan Harold Edick spearheaded the building of a go-cart track in the 1960s. Vince DeVito and Lyle Wagoner (then the mayor) are about to begin a race.

Horse racing also proved a popular sport at Edgewood Park, and an enormous horse barn still exists on the Edgewood property. The sulky was the race of choice. Here, two racers jockey for position in a close call.

Adventure Town was also a popular attraction at Edgewood Park in the 1950s. It was a replica of a town in the Old West, in which actors staged shootouts and bank robberies. There were stagecoach rides, games, and craftsmen demonstrating their techniques at everything from shoeing horses to glass blowing.

This lone cowboy rests a moment to survey the situation as a stagecoach approaches, possibly calculating a holdup.

Edgewood Park and Adventure Town owners Bud Hebert (left) and George Clark (right) stand on either side of a woman identified as Mrs. Barker.

Pirate Bill Johnson, a notorious brigand of the region in the early 1800s and activist during the Patriot War of 1837–1838, was the inspiration for Alexandria Bay's annual Pirate's Weekend. Among the events is a reenactment of a pirate invasion upon the village from the water. This frigate from Kingston, Ontario, was the centerpiece of the waterfront pageant for many years.

Townsfolk prepare for the pirates' onslaught, ready to meet the invasion with firearms, during Pirate's Weekend, held each summer in August.

British forces raise a spyglass from the heights of the Thousand Islands Bridge to witness the impending pirate action during the annual Pirate's Weekend reenactment. In the foreground is W. Grant Mitchell, the person in the center is unidentified, and in the rear is C. B. "Bert" Tidd.

The Alexandria Bay Fire Department has hosted the Firemen's Convention many times over the years. Here, a bucket brigade competes for the best time in this event. These platforms for the competition were generally set up at the lower end of James Street in front of Uncle Sam Boat Tours. The event drew large crowds of spectators.

A race vehicle, the *Wild Geese*, with Garth Van Brocklin at the wheel, competes in a Firemen's Convention event. In the rear are, from left to right, Victor Willix, Terry Millett, and Bud Thomas.

This Small Fry Fishing Derby is a popular event for youngsters from the community, as well as visiting tourists. It takes place each summer at the upper town dock. Van's Motor Marine (in the background) has been a fixture of the Upper Bay since 1946.

The annual antique boat show was originally organized by John Russell *c.* 1978 and still takes place annually at the upper town dock.

In 1948, radio and television star Arthur Godfrey popularized the 1000 Islands and the St. Lawrence River in song with his hit tune "Florence, on the St. Lawrence," also known as "The River Song." In gratitude, he had conferred upon him the title honorary mayor of the 1000 Islands and was given possession of an island in the international rift. Here, Grant Mitchell, president of the Thousand Islands Bridge Authority at the time and prominent hotelier of the village, presents the award to Godfrey during his CBS radio broadcast.

This island in the international rift was presented to Arthur Godfrey in appreciation of his promotion of the 1000 Islands area.

Carmen Basilio, welterweight and lightweight boxing champion, trained in Alexandria Bay in the summers of 1954–1956. Embraced enthusiastically by the community, he was awarded honorary membership in the local Lion's Club. Among the prominent Alexandria Bay businessmen pictured are Frank Cavallario, left, and Lawrence Roy, who is to the right of Basilio (holding the statuette).

An annual fireworks display graces the night sky off the front of the village every Fourth of July and draws thousands of spectators along the shoreline and in boats.

Seven

SPORTS AND PASTIMES

As early as 1845, the Thousand Islands began to gain a name among sportsmen as an ideal fishing destination. Seth Green, a fish culturist, further promoted this when he purchased Manhattan Island, opposite the village, and built what is purported to be the first island cottage on the river. Here, three lucky early-20th-century anglers display their impressive day's catch. They are L. Nick Benson (left), John Kepler (center), and Clay Kepler.

With a little teamwork, this early-1900s couple enjoyed a sizable haul of pike.

Sid Patterson, local bait man and raconteur, displays a nice muskellunge in 1958 at the town dock. The barrels in the boat directly below him carried home the morning haul of bait each day, which were then sold from a little stand at the entrance to the dock.

These fishing guides were adept at not only leading fishing parties to the best fishing grounds but were also able to prepare their catch as a wonderful shore dinner at day's end. They are, from left to right, as follows: (front row) Riley Ledger, Leon Senecal, and Jack Snyder; (back row) Jack Chaltain, Ray Rogers, Dean Senecal, and Jim Duclon.

Frank Cavallario, local restaurateur, displays an enormous muskellunge. These sport fish are known for putting up a tremendous fight, so landing one this size is no small feat.

The environs of the village and river offer an abundance of waterfowl for hunters. These men, showing the results of their efforts one day in 1916, are, from left to right, Sam Guerrieri, Cyril Lee, Fred Blevins, and Alton McCleary.

This hunting party of two had a most impressive shoot on the water. By today's laws, they would be well over the limit.

The Canada goose is a coveted water bird in the region. Orrin La Rue (left) and Harold Houghton spread the wingspan, giving a notion of just how large a bird can be.

Deer hunting has been a popular hunting sport in the region for years. These men, Harry Pickert (left) and Col. Philip Wilhelm, exhibit a fine bounty.

Archie Chase and his son, Willard, offer for inspection the rewards of their trapping efforts, several lush fur pelts.

Shinny, a loosely regulated version of hockey, was a popular pastime for village youth, and a quick game could be set up right on the ice with a little snow removal, a net, and some boards. These fellows enjoy their sport on the Lower Bay, across from the Crossman House, in the early 1900s.

110

Eight
DAILY VILLAGE LIFE

Here on the Upper Bay, three bay gals enjoy an afternoon skate. They are, from left to right, unidentified, Lucille Estes, and Irene Hunt.

Jack Dobbins's store and gas station, at the intersection of Church and Otter Streets, was a popular after-school destination for penny candy in the first half of the 20th century.

Dobbins's store offered an abundance of grocery items and was most often attended by the proprietor's wife, Vivian.

Sports have always been an important part of the community. Programs have been well supported and games well attended. The 1905 Alexandria Bay High School football team poses with the coach. Identified here are the following: ? Comstock (front row, left), Fred Blevins (front row, right), Harold Weller (middle row, third from the left), Hub Comstock (middle row, fourth from the left), Charlie O'Brien (middle row, fifth from the left), and Winfred "Peggy" Northrup (back row, fourth from the left).

Seen here is the 1920–1921 Alexandria Bay High School basketball team. Members of the team are, from left to right, as follows: (front row) Fred Estes; (middle row) Glenn Wilson, Damon Church, John Dobbins, and Howard Marshall; (back row) David Allen (teacher), Sterling Garlock, and Prof. George F. Radley (principal).

In 1960, the Alexandria Central Purple Ghosts were the undefeated league champions.

This Alexandria Bay chapter of the popular girls' organization the Camp Fire Girls posed in the early 1940s for a portrait. Seen here are, from left to right, the following: (front row) Louise Stott, Susanne Massey, Irene Jones, Joyce Petrie, and Ann Rogers; (middle row) unidentified, Betty Rupert, Catherine Petrie, Ada Fitch, Mary House, Una Cornwall, and Beverly Reynolds; (back row) Elizabeth Houghton, unidentified, Florence Fram, Jean Senecal, Mary Lou Griffin, Dorothy Joiner, Regina Pledger, and Madeline House.

Harold Edick's corner pharmacy, on the corner of James and Church Streets, was a mainstay of the village for many years. Pictured are pharmacy employee Alice Cranker Leonard (center) and proprietor Harold Edick (right foreground).

Mrs. Queall maintained a gift shop bearing her name for many decades. (Other popular souvenir stores of the first half of the 20th century included the Nippon Shop, the Japanese Bazaar, and later, La Boutique.) In this view, Queall poses among her items for sale.

Seen is the 1929 Alexandria Bay Boy Scout troop. Members are, from left to right, as follows: (first row) Bill Strough, John Hogan, Keith Ackly, Comeil Allen, and Malcomb Hutchinson; (second row) Jim Pearce, Harry O'Brien, Eddie Roy, Eddie Willis, John Cranker, Frank Aiken, Dick Zoller, Jimmie Heath, and Ray Heath; (third row) Pete Strough, Malcomb Lee, Leo Pharoah, Clarence Collins, Ford Combs, John Rappole, Bud Kenyon, Billy Burtch, Billy Griffin, Harold Keeler, and Ben Cantwell; (fourth row) Rev. Thomas Adams, Norris A. Houghton, and George Hutchinson.

The Alexandria Bay Fire Department is made up of all volunteer firefighters from the community. They give their all in service to their village, and they have been doing so for over 100 years.

The firemen's ball has been an ongoing annual affair for nearly a century. The program for the 1924 ball offers a dance card and pencil to write the partner's name next to the particular style of dance shared.

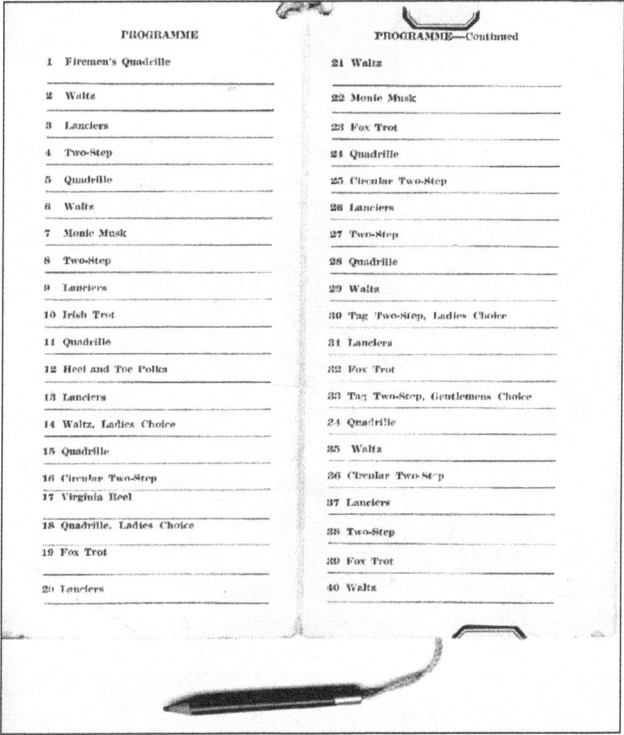

PROGRAMME		PROGRAMME—Continued	
1	Firemen's Quadrille	21	Waltz
2	Waltz	22	Monie Musk
3	Lancers	23	Fox Trot
4	Two-Step	24	Quadrille
5	Quadrille	25	Circular Two-Step
6	Waltz	26	Lancers
7	Monie Musk	27	Two-Step
8	Two-Step	28	Quadrille
9	Lancers	29	Waltz
10	Irish Trot	30	Tag Two-Step, Ladies Choice
11	Quadrille	31	Lancers
12	Heel and Toe Polka	32	Fox Trot
13	Lancers	33	Tag Two-Step, Gentlemens Choice
14	Waltz, Ladies Choice	34	Quadrille
15	Quadrille	35	Waltz
16	Circular Two-Step	36	Circular Two-Step
17	Virginia Reel	37	Lancers
18	Quadrille, Ladies Choice	38	Two-Step
19	Fox Trot	39	Fox Trot
20	Lancers	40	Waltz

This firemen's ball, likely in the 1940s or early 1950s, is exemplary of the kind of strong attendance and good spirit that prevails at the event, a wonderful village tradition.

Some will recognize many of the familiar faces in this *c.* 1960 photograph, which shows a most impressive group of civic-minded protectors of the village.

This blaze two decades ago in the Hartman Block, at the corner of James and Church Streets, destroyed the structure, which housed retail stores and apartments. The building had been erected in 1883 by John Hartman and his son, Henry J. Hartman.

The International Order of Odd Fellows building on Market Street was home to the local newspaper, the *Thousand Islands Sun*, established in 1901. A devastating fire in 1991 (below) forced a move to the current location on Route 12, on the outskirts of the village.

Bingo was once a tent affair, set up out of doors in the fair months as a community entertainment. Ray Rogers enjoys a cigar while he awaits numbers to be called by Joe Marceau.

Tony Folino, a shoemaker and retailer, was born in Guardia Piemontese, Calabria, Italy, in 1905 and immigrated to America in 1925. He opened his first repair shop and shoe store in 1930 on Walton Street in the Ward Block. He moved in 1933 to the location at 43 Church Street that he occupied for 65 years.

Dick Warner (left) and Frank Cavallario sell brooms in 1957 as part of a fund-raising drive for the Lion's Club.

Eugene "Tootie" Gaylord was a village policeman in the 1950s and 1960s, as well as the village water plant manager.

The village cinema was located on Bethune Street, now the site of the Cavallario's Steak House parking lot. The Greek Revival house next door, one of the village's oldest, still exists and remains in the Folino family, which has owned it since *c.* 1950.

In 1932, theatrics of a different sort were taking place during this Daughters of the American Revolution observance of the bicentennial of George Washington's birth.

The members in this early fire department photograph cut a dashing figure in their matching uniforms for most probably a competency competition at a convention.

This undated photograph was taken outside the New Walton Inn on Market Street, which today is an empty lot. On close inspection, the subjects appear to be costumed for a humorous occasion of some sort.

The Fireside Club was a women's study club that evolved from an association with the New York State Federation of Women. Seen in this *c.* 1956 photograph are, from left to right, the following: (front row) Carlene Seeley, Josephine Laurie, Doreen Ruderman, and Jeanne Tague; (back row) Helen MacDonald, Virginia Becker, Carson Case, Doris Langlois, unidentified, and Blanche Gray.

In this early-1960s view, boat-safety-minded men stand around a chart developed to educate the public in on-the-water safety requirements and procedures. Marina owner Ray Rogers is second from the right; his son David (the current proprietor of Rogers Marina) is to his right.

Marjorie Ely, of the 1000 Islands Dance Studio, has been teaching dance in the village for several decades. In this group of student ballerinas, at dress rehearsal for a recital, are, from left to right, Angela Folino, Carolyn McLennan, Kristen Snow, Cindy Cullen, Janice Adderley, and Tina Gleason.

Alexandria Central School is home to an accomplished marching band, seen here en route through the village, with the Monticello Hotel, the old bank building, and Cornwall Brothers in the background. This photograph was taken in the 1960s or 1970s.

High school road trips, particularly the senior trip, have been popular extracurricular events at Alexandria Central School for many years. This group of well-groomed and well-attired students traveled in 1927 to Mount Vernon.

Local businesses sponsored bowling teams that practiced at alleys located within the village. This proud team of the early 1960s displays its trophies. From left to right are Millie Kring, Jo Slocum Megan, Gayle Gaylord Ward, Frank and Connie Cavallario (team sponsors), Sandra Chaltain, and Jessie Newberry.

This 1950s men's bowling team consisted of, from left to right, Orrin La Rue, Royal Garlock, Theron Hartman, Harold Houghton, and Harold Newberry.

This ladies' bowling team, also from the 1950s, included, from left to right, Barbara Britton, Betty Warner, Evelyn Rae, Carmel Folino, and Helen Singer.

The upper town dock was the setting of this romantic interlude for the young couple in this 1960s view.

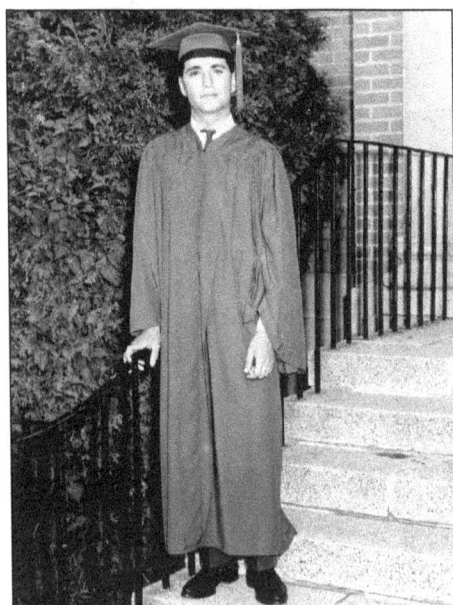

The author, pictured here in 1962, hopes that you have enjoyed your visit to *Alexandria Bay*. Come back again soon.

www.ingramcontent.com/pod-product-compliance
Lightning Source LLC
Chambersburg PA
CBHW080547110426
42813CB00006B/1239